Discovering
A Better Way
To Pray

Steps to Answered Prayers

Deforest L. Augustus

Preface.

This book was written from the aspect of an everyday person. I'm just like you guys and everybody else who have been praying for years and not feeling that I have been getting my prayers answered. Until I started to seek God and to understand the Bible more, my prayers were going to no avail for one, I was praying without faith. For two, I was praying without scripture. And for three I was praying against God's will for my life. Many of us have struggled with the same obstacles when it came to prayer. So over the last couple of years I have grown in my wisdom of the Bible and my relationship with God, and he led me to write this book to help others how to start to build a better relationship with God. This is what this book is all about. Praying to build a better relationship and get your prayers answered according to God's will.

A lot of times we pray out of selfishness, out of hatred, out of greed, out of envy, out of desperation. But God said, "My word is true when you hold steadfast." Learning God's Word to pray will yield you the prayers that you want every single time that you pray, because you are praying according to scripture. You will be praying according to God's will. No matter where you at right now with your faith or your relationship with God, this breaks it down for anybody. New believers, old believers, kids can understand how to have a better prayer life and to get your prayers answered every single time that you play.

So you won't have to struggle with asking people to pray for you every time something goes wrong in your life. You can speak to God directly. You have the same direct line that anyone else has with God to get your prayers answered, to heal the sick, to fix your finances, to stop worrying, discouragement or you name it. Once you finish with this book, you will be able to pray with authority, to just speak to your mountains and know that God is moved on your behalf, because His Word says so and He is true to His Word.

This book also gives after the steps, we go through several different obstacles that we face. And it gives you the scriptures to pray on them, to meditate on them, to understand them so that when you pray, you're praying with authority, you're praying with scripture so that you can overcome or you can get your prayers answered, whatever it is that you may be going through.

I pray that this book blesses you and your family and that you can pass it on to teach somebody else to build a stronger relationship with God and a stronger prayer life to get through the woes and the ups and downs of life. They come at us every single day. Praying, knowing that I can rest in God because His Word says so and that I won't have to worry. I won't have to fret. I will keep my faith and I will trust in the Lord because the Lord is my Savior and my Rock. Prayer in the key to building the relationship with God.

CONTENTS

INTRODUCTION

Ephesians 6:18. NLT

Pray at all times on every occasion in every season in the spirit with all manner of prayer and intriguing. To that end, keep alert and watch with strong purpose and perseverance, interceding in behalf of all the saints, God's concerted people.

This scripture tells us to pray with all types of prayer. Not one type of prayer, it's like the rule basketball and football you can't use improper rules. It's the same thing with prayer. In order for your prayers to be answered, you must pray different types of prayer. Pray with knowing the Scriptures to back the prayer so that when you're praying, your prayers will get answered each and every time according to God's will.

Types of prayer

1. **Prayer of supplication.** Supplication means to petition or entreat someone for something. A passionate zeal and hunger fuse the prayer of supplication. This prayer is a prayer that all Christians should regularly engage in as we earnestly desire to see God's face and to know his will for our life. Tell God that you desire him and hunger for his presence.

2. **Prayer of intercession.** To intercede means to plead or to meditate on behalf of another person. Intercessory prayer means praying the needs of others and seeking God's will for your life. We are called to intercede for others just as Jesus is interceding for us.

3. **Prayer of faith.** The prayer of faith is rooted in our confidence in God's Word. When you are sure that you are praying for God's will, the prayer of faith can be employed. The prayer of faith is knowing God's will, praying it and receiving it and believing that what you are praying for is well and done. Not forgiving and doubting are the two greatest hindrances of prayers of faith.

4. **Prayer of agreement.** The prayer of agreement is when two or more people come together and agree with one another in the Word of God. That

something specific will be done. When we stand together in unity with one purpose, sharing a joint vision and trusting God's Word to be fulfilled. This type of prayer could be considered.

Pray proud, praise and Thanksgiving. Praise and worship brings us into the presence of God. Praising God in both the good and bad times affirms our faith in him. Praise and thanksgiving are powerful weapons. They disarm the two most deadly weapons to our Christian walk, sin/ satanic attacks an unblief, These two things are manifested in many different ways, but praise and thanksgiving is a two-edged sword that helps us fight the evil spirit.

John 15:7. NLT

> *If you live me, abide with me, united to me and my words remain in you and continue to live in your heart, ask for whatever you want and it shall be done for you.*

If your prayers are not answered, it is more of you than it is God. God has given us the tools and the resources to get whatever it is that we desire from God according to his will. So learning to pray according to God's will is essential to get your prayers answered and to live a very successful prayer life, building your relationship with God.

Learning how to pray. It's something most of us were not taught, so we just pray. We go to God with repetition, however it is steps and rules to learn to have a very effective prayer life. God has already given you the means. It's up to you to implement it. Learning the scriptures, learning his promises, living by Word.

When you learn to pray in line with the Word of God, your prayers are answered every single time. It's always yes when you ask God for things according to his will. But learning his will and how to pray is the key to answered prayer.

II Chronicles 7: 14-16.NLT

> *If my people, which are called by my name, shall humble themselves and pray and seek my face and turn from their wicked ways, then I will hear from heaven, and I will forgive them of their sin, and they will heal their land. Now mine eye shall be open and mine ears attent onto the prayers that is made in this place. For now, I have chosen and sanctified this house, that my name may be there forever and mine eyes and mine heart shall be there perpetually.*

If you are not faithful, your prayers will not work. You must have faith in order for you for your prayers to be answered. You cannot pray half-heartedly and expect your prayers to work. It just won't work. You must pray and be faithful in your prayers. Having faith while praying is a key for your prayers to begin to work.

Now, if you follow these steps, your prayers will be answered every single time that you pray.

STEP 1

A. Decide what you want from God, and get the Scriptures that promise the things that you want. Faith begins where the will of God is known.

When you are praying, you must know the Scriptures to have faith in to begin to get your prayers answered.

If you don't know the Scriptures, you can't expect your prayers to be answered because you're praying amiss. God has given us the tools. He has given us the Scriptures and the promises. It is up to us to get the Scriptures that we need for what we are praying for in order to get God to answer our prayers. Without having the Scriptures to back what we are praying, we are praying amiss. And more than likely your prayers will not get answered. So learn the Scriptures you need for the things that you are praying for so that your prayers can be answered every single time that you pray.

B. Get the promises of the Scriptures fixed in your heart, not only in your mind.

You must meditate on them. Take time to meditate on the Scriptures for the things that you are praying for. Meditating is learning the Scriptures, putting them inside of your heart not just in your mind. And you meditate on it, and you remind God of the things that he has promised you. So when you're praying, you're praying knowing that God has already given you the things that you need. Now you're just commanding God to release them to you.

Meditating on the Scriptures is a key element. Right under having faith to get your prayers answered. Because meditation builds faith. When you begin to meditate on God's Word and learning his Word and learning the Scriptures, when you're praying, you begin to pray with authority, and now you're not just praying out of fear or out of hope that your prayers may get answered. You've put these Scriptures into your heart, so now that you know what you are praying for.

C. Be ready to use the Scriptures on devils and demons.

Speak the Scriptures against all attacks. When you learn these Scriptures, when you find the Scriptures and learn these Scriptures into your heart, when things come up, you can speak the Scriptures back against him. The same as Jesus did when he went out to fast for 40 days into the wilderness and the devil attacked him. Jesus fought back with Scripture. Scripture that he just meditated on while he was in the wilderness building and praying to God.

So when the enemy comes, knowing the Scriptures is going to be your sword to fight against the negative thoughts, the negativity that may come against you after you have prayed. Use the Scriptures to fight those demons, to remind the devil to free, to remind the devil to run from you. And he will run because you know the Scriptures. You know God's promises and you know that God will come through every single time according to his Word.

Too many people say, "*If God wanted me to have it, he will give it to me.*" *This is not correct. God has given us the things that we need to have a successful life. In prayer, health and finances, everything in your life, but learning the Scriptures and meditating on them and learning how to use them in prayer and in attacks from the enemy is a key element to building a successful prayer life.*

Learn the Scriptures and God will give you the things that he has promised. Meditate on them day and night. Do not sleep on building your relationship with God through prayer and meditation on the Scriptures, on his Word.

STEP 2

Ask God for what you want? Ask God for what you want, not what you want for someone else, not for what someone else wants.

God knows what you want before you ask, but you still have to ask. And asking God for things you want is important according to his will. When you know God's will and what Scripture says about things, when you're asking for things, you're asking for things that you know God has already given you. You can't ask for things that are not according to God's will.

For example, you can't ask for another person's spouse, husband or wife or things like that. Or things that will hurt you or things that will hurt someone else or so be it. You have to ask for things according to God's will. But when you ask according to his will and in faith, the answer will always be yes.

Will it always be immediate? No, but that is where faith comes in. Faith comes in knowing that you will receive what you pray for according to God's will no matter how long it takes for it to come into fruition.

Mark 11:24 NLT.

> *I tell you, you can pray for anything, and if you believe that you received it, it will be yours. You must believe that you received it. Pray, believe, and you will receive the things according to God's will. But if you're praying and you don't think that you're going to get the things that you're praying for, nine times out of 10 you won't get them because you're praying without faith in the things that you're praying for.*

So you can't pray and hope that God is going to give you the things that you're asking for. You must know without a doubt in your mind that God is going to give you the things that you want. This is faith. Praying in faith is knowing that you're going to get the things that you asked for according to God's will.

You can't waiver in your belief that, "Oh well, maybe he'll give it to me. Maybe he won't." You must pray and believe that God will give you the things that you were praying for and you will receive them. They will be yours according to God's will.

Philippians 4: 19.NLT

And this same God, who takes care of me, will supply all your needs from his glorious riches which have been given to us in Christ Jesus.

God will take care of all of your needs. You do not have to worry. When you pray for things, God wants to give them to you. This Scripture is talking about money. It's talking about wealth and health and all of the fruits of the spirit. When you pray, knowing that God is glorious and he wants to supply your needs, you will receive the things that you were praying for. Not only is that you're praying in faith and belief, God will supply the things that you need. He will not lack in anything that he promises us.

Romans 4:20-22 NLT

Abraham never wavered in believing God's promises. In fact grew stronger, and in this he brought glory to God. He was fully convinced that God is able to do whatever he promises, and because of Abraham's faith, God counted him as righteous.

See, God told Abraham he will be the father of many nations. Even at Abraham's old age with no children, Abraham believed in God. So just imagine you're 100 years old, and God tells you, "Hey, I'm going to make you a nation, a father of many nations."

But you're like, "Hey God, I don't even have any kids and I'm 100 years old. So I'm way past the years of bearing, and my wife is past the years of bearing as well. So how can I have kids?"

But God says, "Trust me." And Abraham trusted God. Humanly speaking, it was impossible, but with God, anything is possible. And Abraham believed, and God blessed Abraham with many nations at an old age where it was humanly speaking impossible to bear kids. But God fulfilled his promise, and Abraham lived to be the father of many nations from the promises that God gave him. And Abraham did not waver in his faith.

He believed God at his word. The same is for you. God is promising you success, health, wealth, all of the fruits of the spirit. You must believe, and when you're praying, pray in belief, but also know the promises that you are playing for and God will be true to his word and fulfill everything that he promises you.

John 20:24-25 NLT

> . One of the 12 disciples, Thomas, was not with the others when Jesus came. They told him, "We have seen the Lord." But he replied, "I won't believe it unless I see the nail wounds in his hand. Put my fingers in

them and place them into the wound and placed them into the wound in his side."

Thomas only wanted to believe once he saw. Thomas did not have the faith that God was speaking about. See, some people won't believe until they see the things coming to fruition already. Oh yeah, now I believe because I have it. Now I believe because I'm healed. Now I believe because my bills are paid. Now I believe because I have money. Now I believe because I feel better because I could see it. But God is asking you to have faith and believe before you can even see the things that you are praying for come into pass. You must believe before you see them. You must believe before you see them to have the blessing that God has for you.

Romans 4:17.

> *This is what the Scripture means when God told him, "I have made you the father of many nations." This happened because Abraham believed in God, who brings back the dead to life and who creates new things out of nothing.*

Abraham believed God because he knew that God was powerful and he was true to his word. It's a difference between the faith of Thomas and the faith of Abraham. People pray to get Abraham's blessings with Thomas's faith, but it won't work like that. You must have Abraham's faith to get Abraham's blessing. You can't walk around and think that you won't believe God at his word until you can see it, until it is there for you already. You must believe before it is there, before you can see it, before you can touch it, before you can feel it.

The same as Abraham, who was an old man, who was past the age of bearing, but God made a way for him and his wife to have a son, to leave all of the blessings that God left for Abraham. Nations, money, family, everything that God left for Abraham, he believed and he received it.

When you pray and believe, then you receive not when you get then you believe. You must believe you received them before you can even see it. Before you even know where it's coming or how it's coming, or how you are going to get it. You must pray and believe that you've already received it. Then you will be blessed. Then you will receive what God has for you.

Pray and believe like Abraham. Don't be like Thomas. The Bible doesn't refer back to having faith like Thomas. He gave us the example not to have faith like Thomas, and Thomas was a disciple right next to Jesus. Everyone else believed except for Thomas. Don't be Thomas. Learn to be Abraham. Learn to believe and receive and you will get the things that you are praying for according to God's riches, according to God's promise, according to God's glory for your life.

STEP 3

Let every thought and desire affirm you got what you asked. Never permit a mental picture of failure to be in your mind. Think on victory, don't think on defeat.

Because once you start to think defeat, you become defeated. But if you fix your mind on the victory and the promises of God, you can have the things that you're praying and believing for. See, the devil comes to distract you, and get you off track, to let you know, "Hey, you're not going to be able to get that. That's not going to work for you. You're still not going to make it. You're still not going to be able to do it."

But you must think on the positive things and not let any negative pictures come and stay in your mind. They will come, but this is why you use the scriptures to fight against those negative thoughts. When they do come get your mind on what God said, not on what your thoughts say, not on what your eyes see. Because your thoughts and your eyes will fail you every time. But God's word is true and it's always relevant and he sticks to his word.

Philippians 4:6-8 NLT

> *Don't worry about a thing. Instead, pray about everything. Tell God what you need and thank him for all he has done. Then you will experience God's peace which exceeds anything we can understand. His peace will guard your heart and your mind as you live in Christ Jesus. And now dear brothers and sisters. One final thing. Fix your thoughts on what is true and honorable and right and pure and lovely and admirable. Think about things that are excellent and worthy of praise.*

The Bible tells us that we must think on the good things of God. Think on God's promises. Don't think on the negative. Don't think on the doubt. Don't think on the disbelief. Think on the things that God has promised us. That way when you pray, you're praying in faith and you're staying in faith because you're not letting negative thoughts conquer you. Once you begin to let these negative thoughts conquer you, they sink into your heart and then they bring on disbelief. So God said, you must think on things that are good, pure and lovely. Think on that. When you pray this, think on the things that you are praying for. Don't think on what can go wrong, or what may not go wrong, or what may not happen. God doesn't command us that. Think on good things, good things only.

Songs 91:16 NLT,

> *I will reward them with long life and give them my salvation. Don't give in to the devil so easily. He will fight you all the way. God has rewarded you with his salvation of victory and all the things that you're believing for. But the devil wants to come and fight you and attack your thoughts. See, in order to change your life, you must change your thoughts. This is what this is talking about. Don't think on the negative things that are going to come. Because negative things are going to come, you cannot stop them. But you can control what stays in your mind.*

You can't stop a bird from passing by and pooping on your head, but you can stop a bird from coming and planting their nest. That you can stop. So know, all kind of negativity is going to come our way. And that is the enemy attacking your thoughts. Do not allow the enemy to attack your thoughts. Continue to think on the things that God has promised you. Think on that. You can believe God to keep your faith. Once you begin to believe God and his word, you will be able to keep your faith. No matter what you're praying for, no matter what you're going through, you will be able to keep the faith, and keep knowing that God is your source, and that all things will work themselves out. Do not think on negative things and bad things when you pray.

James 1: 26-27 NLT

> *If you claim to be religious but do not control your tongue, you are fooling yourself and your religion is worthless. Pure and genuine religion is the sight of God the father. Means caring for orphans, and widows in their distress, and refusing to let the world corrupt you. When you're praying, you must check yourself and not only speak God's word, but be a living testimony to God's work, doing good things, helping others, being positive, believing, being genuine in your faith. It doesn't help you to talk about God and go out and live a negative lifestyle, a lifestyle that is not the selfish or self centered, and all of these things that bring on negative discord into your spirit.*

God wants us to walk and be an example for others, so that we can live God's word and fulfill our purpose. So when you're praying for things and you're praying for things according to God's will, be sure that you are living the life that God wants us to live. Doing the thing that God wants us to do, not out here being negative or hateful towards other people like we tend to be. Help others, control your tongue, control your anger. That is a big, big, big problem that we have, our tongue. The tongue is very powerful. The tongue speaks life and death.

But learn to speak life with your tongue. Learn to control your thoughts and watch how every time you pray your prayers are answered. God will not answer your prayers long as you're praying according to his will, being genuine in your thoughts and in your life. Living by an example so that when other people see you, they can see God. Because, you may be the only person that ... you may be the only guy that some people see. So living the life, controlling your thoughts, controlling your tongue, is the key to living a successful spiritual life. Growing spiritually to God.

What you believe and what you think is I must say, 80% of the fight. If you believe God and his word, and you think on good things, you will have a successful prayer life. Your prayers will begin to be answered. Your life will begin to change. You will be able to receive the abundance that God has for you, that God has for everyone, that God has for all of us. If you learn to control your thoughts, to control your thoughts is to control your life. So when you're praying, pray and believe and don't let nothing come in between that. Yes, the enemy will attack it every angle, but continue to believe that God's true in his word and his promises are real and they are for you, which they are. Get his promises, meditate on them, think on them and continue to grow.

STEP 4

God against every evil that comes in the minds. Stay away from all places, and things that will not support your affirmation that God has answered your prayer.

You can control what you think on. You have to stay away from people, places and things that will go against what you believe in. So let's say God spoke to you, and you go out and talk to one of your friends or your family members, and they may be a negative person. They may give you a negative response. And it can hurt the way that you look at things based on who it is, and how they respond to the things that you're sharing with them, or the things that's going on in your life. You must guard your heart and your thoughts.

Stay away from people who will not support you, who will not help you grow, who will not be pushing you towards the things that God has for you.

Because, that is very important. It is easy to go around someone, and they put you in a bad spirit because of the way that they think, and the way that they talk about the things that you're doing. Sometimes the things that you have going on, God did not want everybody to know. Sometimes you just got to do it. So if there's someone that you may go around, or it's a place, or it's a habit that will inhibit to you from God's will, you have to remove yourself. You have to guard yourself and put yourself in places that will support your affirmation that your prayers have been answered. Stay away from things that will not support that.

Philippians 4:8 NLT

> *And now dear brothers and sisters, one final thought. Fix your thought on what is true, and honorable, and right, and pure, and lovely, and admirable. Think about things that are excellent and worthy of praise. You can help what you think on. What you put inside of you is what comes out, right? So if you watch a bunch of negative TV shows, and listen to a bunch of negative movies, or watch a bunch of negative music, or hang around a bunch of negative people, that will tend to come out of you in your spiritual life.*

So you have to put yourself in places that's going to nourish your spirit, that's going to feed your spirit, that's going to give to you, and not take away. See there's so many things that want to take away from you, but you must put yourself in places where things that are going to feed your spirit, not take away from you. This is what this is talking about. You can help the things that you think on once you put yourself in the right environment, the right soil to grow. Is just like a tree. When you put it in the fertile soil, a tree is going to grow, a plant is going to grow. But if you put it at rocky, and thorny unhealthy soil, it won't grow. Or if it grow, it's going to grow handicap. Or it's not going to grow in the way that it wasn't supposed to grow.

Thoughts are governed by observations, associations, and teachings. What is governing your thoughts? What are you around that can be hindering you and your thoughts? You have to remove yourself from these things immediately in order to grow and have a very successful spiritual life. So we can't walk around and do the things that everybody else ... Yes, it may be fun. It may be funny, it may be all of ... it might be entertaining. But if it's not something that's going to feed your spirit and support your answered prayers, you must remove yourself away from it.

Same as associations. You can't associate with people or things that are not going to push forward your spiritual walk and in your prayer life. You must put yourself around people who are going to support you and believe you in the things that you have going on your mission to grow closer to God. Stay away from places and things that do not support that. That is evil. That is from the devil. That's how the devil gets you. He wants to plant a seed of doubt. So you won't believe that God has answered your prayers. God has brought you to the place that he wants you. The devil wants you to deny it and doubt it. And once you begin to doubt, that is what is considered unfaithful, not having faith. And now your prayers are being hindered. Because you're praying and you don't have any faith or you fail to let ... So you must believe before you even see it.

Numbers 13: 25-33 NLT

After exploring the land for 40 days, the men returned to Moses, Aaron, and the whole community of Israel at Kadesh in the wilderness of Paran. They reported to the whole community what they had seen and showed them the fruit they had taken from the land. This was their report to Moses. We entered the land you sent us to explore it. It indeed is it bountiful country, a land flowing with milk and honey. Here is the common fruit it produces. But the people living there are powerful and their towns are large and fortified. We even saw giants there, the descendants of Anak. The Amalekites, and the Negev, the Hittites and the Jebusites and the Amorites live in the hill country. The Canaanites live on the coast of the Mediterranean sea and along the Jordan Valley.

But Caleb tried to quiet the people as they stood before Moses, let's go at once to take the land. He said, we can certainly conquer. But the other man who had explored the land with him disagreed. We can't go up against them. They are stronger than we are. So they spread the bad report about the land among the Israelites. The land we traveled through and explored will devour anyone who goes to live there. All the people we saw were huge. We even saw giants there, the descendants of Anak. Next to them, we are like grasshoppers. And that's what they thought too.

See this is a bad report. Moses knew that we can conquer it, but he sent these people to scape the land, and they come back and given a bad report. "Oh, these giants are huge. We can't take them. They are much stronger than us." This is the same thing with life. You might go to the doctor and they might give you a bad report, and you begin to believe it. You began to let it sink into your spirit that, "Hey, maybe this is going to be bad for me." And you begin to accept it. And so once you begin to accept it, you begin to bring it to life.

But God said that I come to conquer and to give you the land, and to give you peace, to give you wealth. But when you come back, bringing bad reports, you begin to doubt God. And then, you begin to have disbelief which causes unfaithfulness. And so, your prayers won't be answered. Yes. When you look at things through your eyes, "Oh my goodness, these giants are huge." Or whatever the negative thought may be. When you look with your eyes, and not with your heart, and not with the scriptures, yes, you will begin to doubt. But when you fill yourself with the promises and the faith of God, you can conquer anything.

So when you pray, you pray with authority, you know your prayers will be answered because you believe no matter what you see, no matter what you hear, no matter how the circumstances may look, God is your conqueror and you will come out on top. Praying according to his will and having faith, we walk by faith and not by sight. Sight produces an evil report. Be careful of what you allow into your consciousness, what you allow to manifest into your consciousness because it will begin to leave you with doubt.

Numbers 14:9 NLT.

Do not rebel against the Lord and do not be afraid of the people of the land. They are only helpless prey to us. They have no protection, but the Lord is with us. Don't be afraid of them. See God is telling you, "Yes, it may look like they're bigger, it may look like they're stronger, but I am your source, I am your victory, I am your strength. Don't doubt." And fear will rob you of the blessings and the things that God has for you.

You cannot let doubt and fear arouse and stay in your life. Yes, doubt and fear may come, but you must attack it with the promises and the things that God has given you. Study the scriptures, meditate on the scriptures, put the scriptures into your heart, not just into your mind. So when doubt and fear comes, you can fight it. So you won't weary, you won't get weak, because you know who your God is and you will stay strong and faithful. Love never fails and faith will always overcome. That is a promise of God.

STEP 5

A. Meditate constantly on scriptures. See yourself for what you asked for.

B. Make plans according, as if it was already a reality.

C. Meditating on the scriptures is the key to getting the scriptures into your heart.

How do you meditate? If you have to sit down in a quiet place, cut off all distractions with your Bible, highlight the scriptures, write them down, whatever you may need to do. And read them and meditate on them. See them, feel them, as you dwell in God's presence. This is where pray for understanding and guidance as you read his word and meditate on it.

Just like you meditate on bad things that happened in your life, it's the same thing with meditating on scripture and good things. When something's going wrong, and you sit there, and you just constantly think about it. Well, do that with the scriptures that you are believing for, the things that you are praying for. So that you can grow strong in your faith, and in your relationship with God. See, you have to see yourself with the things that you've already asked for. Seeing it is a very key part. When you pray, you already have to see yourself having it. You can't let doubt and disbelief come and manifest into your thoughts, into your life. Seeing it before it's there. That's where the faith takes place.

You pray for something that you just see and it makes you smile. It makes you happy because you know that that is good every single time. And his answer is always yes. According to his will. Praying and seeing it in your heart is the key. Make plans as if it's already yours. So let's say you're believing that you're going to have a big house, and let's say that you give yourself a timestamp of when this is going to happen or whatever it may be. Make plans like, "You know what, when I get this big house next year, I'm going to have Christmas at my house. Y'all will come to my house next year for Christmas." Some people like, "Well, you ain't got a house yet." But don't worry about it. But next Christmas I'm going to have this house. Y'all are going to be at my house for Christmas.

Just to give you an example. Just make plans for the things that you want. If you're planning to be married, or have a better job, whatever it may be that you're believing for, even health. You might be going through some type of sickness ... And you know what? Next month I'm going to get outside and I'm going to run. If something's wrong with you physically. I'm going to walk down a street. Yes, I may still be hurting. I might still be in this bed, but I'm already seeing myself. I'm already making plans that next month I'm going to be outside. Next month I'm going to be outside walking. Next month I'm going to be out there planting a garden or whatever it is that you may want to do. Make plans as if it's already yours. You just waiting on it to show up.

Proverbs 4:20-22 NLT

> *My child, pay attention to what I say. Listen carefully to my words. Don't lose sight of them. Let them penetrate deep in your heart for they bring life to those who find them and healing to the whole body. God's word is the written word. Once you get it and put it inside you, it becomes the living word. Now you working with what you need. Now you have your ammunition to go out in it, and fight the enemy, fight the negative thoughts. But you must have God's word inside you and keep them deep in your*

heart. Because they bring life to you. This is your source. This is your power, the word of God. God says, "Put my words first, inclined ears onto my sayings. Don't let them depart before your eyes, because my words are life."

God's word is life. It is your life. It is your prayer life. It is your daily life. Put God's word into your heart and believe it. Let it sink deep inside from meditating on the scriptures day and night. God says, "Pray continuously." How do you pray continuously? You pray continuously by always thinking on the good and pure thoughts that God has for you. You pray continuously by staying in God's presence, by allowing God to lead you with every decision and aspect of your life. This is how you continue to grow in God.

If you found the scriptures for what you were praying for, you can see what you're asking for. So if you're asking for finances, you find the scriptures on finances. You're praying for health. If you're praying about disappointment or discouragement, you find the scriptures, you find the promises, and you stand on top of them until you have what it is that you are praying for. That's how you begin to receive and get your prayers answered. Find the scriptures. Whatever you are going through, the Bible has the answers for you. Search the Bible, study the Bible, read the Bible. It's there for you. It's there for the taker.

God has given us everything that we need. It's up to us to use it, but how do you use it? You must first discover it. Once you discover it, you begin to seek knowledge and then God will give you the knowledge that you're seeking, but you must begin to seek it. You must begin to believe. You must begin by putting the scriptures inside you so that you can have the faith that you need to pray, to believe, to walk by faith and not by sight so that your life will yield the fruit. You will be able to have all the fruits of the spirit that God has for us. Once you begin to meditate and continue to think on the things that God has given us, he will make his word good if you stand by it. Learn his word so you can stand by it, so it would become a part of you. Your life will begin to change, your family will begin to change, the way that you think, the way that you see things will begin to change once you stand by God's word.

Mark 11:23-24 NLT

> *I tell you the truth, you can say to this mountain, may you be lifted up and thrown into the sea and it will happen. But you must really believe it will happen and have no doubt in your heart. I tell you, you can pray for anything and if you believe that*

you received it, it will be yours. You must pray and believe that you received it. Get the scriptures for the things that you were seeking, so that you can receive them. God is here to give them to you. God wants us to be blessed. God wants you to be financially free. He wants you to be healthy. He wants you to have a sound mind and spirit. He wants you to prosper. He wants you to give. He wants you to be a vessel he can use to bless other people, but you must put his word inside you.

You must believe and not have doubt. See the things that you're praying for to happen. You can move mountains. You can heal yourself. You can change your finances. All of these are the fruits of the spirit that God has given you, but you must get it inside you to get it out of you. So when the enemy is attacking you, you have the tools, you have the amour of God on you already, because you put the armor of God on you. This is a spiritual war that we are fighting, and the fight is a spiritual war. You must amour yourself with God's word and God's will for your life. Then you come out on top every single time. And every time that you pray you will know what you're praying for and your prayers will always be answered. You won't have to wait around and wonder. Your prayers will be answered every single time.

STEP 6

Think on the greatness of God and his goodness. Count your blessings and faith will increase. Lift your heart to God constantly in gratitude, and increasing praise for what he has done, and what he is now doing. Think on the greatness that God has given you, thank him for the things that he has done.

God has done so much already. He deserves all your praise no matter what. No matter what. If he did nothing else for you from this day forth, he deserves all your praise for all the things that he has done. You must increase your praise by thanking God, thanking him for his goodness. Thanking him for the goodness that he is already done.

Life is filled with so many obstacles and problems that we tend to drift away from the things that God has already done, because of the new things that we're facing. Because we're seeing them with our eyes and not with our heart, not with God's promises. So we begin to forget and not think on the things that God has already done. Think about how many times God has already gotten you through situations and circumstances that you don't know how you got out of. But God has delivered you every single time. When something's going wrong, begin to think on the things that God has already done. Think on the things that God is already doing. Think on the things that has already happened. How many mountains you have climbed on the top every single time. Yes, we may go through heartache and disappointment along the way, but God is always faithful and true. He will always come through for you no matter what. He will always come through.

I have to stop and remind myself of the things that God has done for me when obstacles come, when life hits you in the face, when you get the unexpected. Loss of job or loss of health, loss of a family member, and all of these devastating things, loss of finances. And you begin to worry about the things that are in front of you. But God says, "Don't worry. The lilies in the field don't worry, the birds don't worry, I take care of them. So how much more will I take care of you?" Remind yourself of God's goodness right now.

Think of the things that God has done. Write them down. Think of all the obstacles that God has taken you through. Think of all the greatness God is. Think of all the things that God has done. And once you begin to think on it and see, you begin to have a different perspective, you begin not to worry. You begin to see that God is always faithful and true. Think on the things that God has brought you through. I know it's so many things you probably can't even think of. This thing that God blocked you from that you didn't even see coming that you don't know to this day could have hurt you and hindered you. The enemy tries to attack you, but because God is with you, he is always working for your good so that you can live in his purpose and his will for your life. But you must take the time to thank him and appreciate him for the things he has already done.

Philippians 4:8 NLT

And now dear brothers and sisters, one final thought. Fix your thought on what is true and honorable, and right and pure, and lovely and admirable. Think about the things that are excellent and worthy of praise. Think about the things that are worthy. Think about things that are lovely. We all have tough times and we all have good times. But when we look at the world through the world standard, we begin to weigh the tougher times heavier than the good times. God is like, "Look at how many times I come through for you."

Just like Jesus and the disciples, right? All of the things that the disciples was able to firsthand witness Jesus do, it was still times where they didn't understand. That they couldn't see the miracles he's done. And so Jesus will be like, "Haven't you saw all the things that I've done? I'm not going to be with y'all forever. Yeah, I have been living off of milk, but it's time now to live off of meat. I need y'all to go out here and teach." They were right there next to him, but couldn't see the things that he was doing. They couldn't see it.

Don't be like the disciples in the negative way. Let me say it. Believe God, thank him for the things he's done. Pay attention for the things that he has done already. He has done so many marvelous and wonderful things already in your life. You do not have to worry. You do not have to stress about anything that comes up in your life. Think on all the times that he has got you through.

Mark 9:22 NLT

The spirit often throws him into the fire or into water trying to kill him. Have mercy on us and help us if you can. "What do you mean if I can?" Jesus asks. Anything is possible if a person believes. The father instantly cried out, I do believe, but help me overcome my unbelief. Jesus is telling us right here I can do anything. It is nothing too big for me. All you have to do is believe. Focus your mind on the good things God has done and the good things that he's going to already do in your life. He is already doing it. He is already making provisions for whatever it is that you were praying for. For whatever it is that you're believing, God is already making provisions. Just believe him. Take him at his word. He is lovely. He loves you and he wants you to prosper, and to answer your prayers every single time.

STEP 7

Make every prayer relative to what you asked for, a statement of faith instead of unbelief. Now when you pray, you pray with the scriptures, so you petition God for the things that you believe in.

It's just liked a lawyer going to court. You pay a lawyer because they've been to school and they've studied the law, so they know the laws. So when you go to God and you know the laws, and you know the promises, and you know the scripture, you pray and you command what's already yours. Blessings are already yours. Faith is already yours. Health is already yours. Finances is already yours. Prosperity is already yours. All these things are already yours. So when you pray and you ask, you don't continue to ask and ask and ask. That is unbelief. You pray and you thank him for the things that he's already done.

So, you pray once, whatever it is that you're praying for, you praying with description, but then you come back and you reaffirm it with scripture. Thank you, God, for healing me. The Bible says that I am healed. You reaffirm, and you don't continue to ask. When you continue to ask, that is a prayer of unbelief. You can think thoughts of faith just as well as you can think unbelief. Condition yourself to think of faith, to think of the things that God wants you to have because he's already given it to us. Jesus died so that we can have these things. But you must first learn the scriptures to understand and receive the things of the spirit that God wants to give you.

Thinking faith thoughts, and speaking faith words. That's how you do it. Think of the faith. Think of the promises. Speak the promises. When things come up, you speak the promises. You don't speak the unbelief. You don't speak the doubt. You speak the promises that God has already given you, and it will be yours every single time. Think on the things that God has promised us, God has given us so much. God loves you. God wants you to prosper. He has given it to you. He sent his son so that we can have all the prosperity, so then we can defeat the enemy, so that we can live abundantly, so that we can help him bless each other. God wants you healed. God wants you blessed. God wants you stress free. These are promises of the spirit. This is promises of God's word. Get into these promises. Get into God's word. Pray, believe, meditate, pray on the scriptures, meditate on the scriptures.

If you prayed and claim God heard you, then when you pray, don't ask for it the way you did the first time. It's already yours. He's already answered you the first time. Just keep reaffirming when you're praying, thank him for what you praying for. If you pray for a new job, you thank him for the job even though you maybe can't see it just yet. Thank God for the job already. Thank him for all that he has done. Thank him and love him. Don't ask again. Pray it in faith. Remind the Lord you're praying. You believe him and thank him for your answers. Just when you know the scriptures, you just remind the guy, "Hey God, you said that I could have this. So I'm just reminding you that I'm believing and I have faith that it's coming. I'm just reminding you that I'm still believing and I know that it's coming. Thank you, father God."

See now you have prayed and stayed in faith. Now your prayers are being answered because you're praying and you know that God will answer your prayers. You know that God loves you and he wants your prayers to be answered. See, that's the difference. You're not steady asking, you're not steady wondering. See, when you praying and asking, asking. It's like, "Oh Lord, I don't know if he's going to do it. So I'm going to keep asking because that feels like the right thing to do." But when you know the scriptures, and you know the promises, you know that God is faithful to his word and he cannot lie to you.

So your prayers must be answered when you know his word according to the scripture. So if you pray seven times for anything you pray six times out of unbelief if you steady asking God the same thing over and over and over. Pray with affirmation, pray with authority, pray with the scriptures, pray with the promises, and your prayers will be answered every single time. When you believe, you enter into rest. So when you pray and you believe that's it, you rest. You don't worry, you don't stress. When negativity comes to your mind, you continue to speak faith. You continue to speak life over the situation. You do not worry yourself. You rest. Faith is resting, rest in God.

God wants us to rest in him. So when you're praying, get the scriptures, meditate the scriptures, put the scriptures in your heart. Think on things that you pray for. Don't let negative thoughts come into your mind. Speak it. Put yourself in situations that's going to grow your faith and bold your spirit. Don't put yourself in a situation that's going to hinder you and not reaffirm the things that God has promised. Get the promises of God inside of you, and every time that you pray, you will have answered prayers. I better wait to pray answered prayers.

HEALING SCRIPTURES

It is God's will for you to be healed.

James1:5-8. "If you seek wisdom, ask our generous God and He will give it to you. He will not rebuke you for asking. But when you ask, be sure that your faith is in God alone; do not waver. A person with divided loyalties is uncertain as a wave of the sea that is blown and tossed by the wind. Such people should not expect to receive anything from the Lord. Their loyalty is divided between God and the world. They are unstable in everything that they do."

When you are praying and declaring healing, because God gave us the power to heal. He didn't ask us to be healed, He told us to heal the sick, heal the weak. You must believe to receive your healing. You can't waiver. You can't pray for healing and continue to take medicine and believe whatever the doctor report says. You must believe what God says, that you are healed and that you are well.

1 John 5:15. *"And since we know He hears us when we make our requests, we also know that He will give us what we asked for."*

When you were praying and declaring victory over your life, God wants to give it to you, it is yours, it is yours for the taking. All you have to do is have faith and believe that you are healed, believe that your family member is healed. But it takes faith on both ends when praying for healing for someone. But, you can heal yourself, God can do miraculous and wonderful things in healing . Jesus Christ is the same yesterday, today and forever. God does not control everything. He won't hurt you to heal you. That's not how God works.

Satan has the power of death, but God gave us the power over the devil, to rebuke the devil. God gave us the power to heal a sickness and disease. God does not control, He gave us the power. So use your power to heal, to deliver, to bring back from the dead. God gave you the power to do it, but you must believe in order to receive the blessing. "I pray that your ..."

Ephesians 1:18-19 NLT

"I pray that your hearts will be flooded with light so that you can understand the confident hope He has given to those He has called. His Holy people who are His rich and glorious inheritance. I also pray that you understand the incredible greatness of God's power for us who believe in Him."

This is the same mighty power dwelling inside you to heal, to deliver, to raise from the dead. Learn to use your power through meditation and faith. With faith, you can move mountains, you can heal yourself, you can heal people, you can raise people from the dead. This is what God gave us when Jesus Christ died on the cross. He gave us the power to move mountains, to heal. Use your power, meditate, build your faith so that you can heal.

Philippians 1:6 NLT,

"And I am certain that God who began the good work within you, will continue His work until it is finally finished on the day that Christ returns."

Often that God is with you. Know that He is with you through whatever journey that you are taking concerning your health, or the health of a family member. Have faith and know that you have the power because God gave it to you, and God is with you to guide you, to heal you and health in your life. All you have to do is speak it and believe it, and the healing is yours.

Ephesians 2:8-9 NLT

> *"God saved you by His grace when you believe, and you don't take the credit for that, it is a gift from God. Salvation is not a reward for the good things we have done so none of us can boast about it."*

Grace and salvation is the strength and the power of God, so that you can heal yourself, God wants you healed, God wants you well, this is why God gave us these things as a gift, you didn't earn it, but it's yours, use it.

Mark 6:5 NLT

> *"And because of their unbelief He couldn't do any miracles among them except, to place His hands on a few sick people and heal them." Even Jesus couldn't do miracles to people who didn't believe, but He healed those who believed. If you believe Him for healing for yourself, for anybody all it takes is faith, and you can and will be healed.*

It's millions of people who get up every single day, from their most sickness and chronic diseases, and believe and speak healing over their life, and they are healed, they are walking today. Just have faith and you can be healed.

1 Peter 2:24 NLT

"He personally carried all sin in His body on the cross, so that we can be dead to sin and live for what is right. By His wounds, you are healed." You are healed. God has gave the ultimate sacrifice through Jesus Christ that you can be healed. All you have to do is speak it and believe it. You don't have to pray for healing. Touch yourself, you are healed. Speak healing, believe healing and have faith and you are healed.

Matthew 10 NLT

Jesus called His 12 disciples together and gave them the authority to cast out evil spirits and heal every kind of illness."

You are a disciple of Jesus. We are the apostles. God gave us the power to heal, so use it. Don't pray for healing, heal yourself, heal others, but you must have faith in order for healing to be activated. You have the power, heal.

Acts 3:16 NLT,

"Through faith in the name of Jesus, this man was healed." You know how crippled he was before. Faith in Jesus name has healed him before your very eyes.

The kingdom of heaven is here. God has given us the power to heal; have faith and be healed.

Ephesians 1:3 NLT

> *"All praise to God, the Father of our Lord Jesus Christ who has blessed us with every spiritual blessing in the heavenly realms, because we are united with Christ.*

You've already got it, you already have everything that you need. Believing in Jesus Christ, filled with the Holy Spirit, you have healing power in your body. Have faith and use it. Romans 8:9, "But you are not controlled by your sinful nature, you are controlled by the spirit. If you have the spirit of God living in you, and remember that those who don't have the spirit of Christ living in them, do not belong to Him."

You have the spirit of God in you, you have healing power. You have the power that Jesus used to heal many sick and many people of diseases, have faith and be healed.

Acts 3:7-8 NLT

> *"Then Peter took the lame man by the right hand and helped him up. As as he did the man's feet and ankles were instantly healed and strengthened. He jumped up and stood to his feet and began to walk. Then walking, leaping and praising God, he went into the temple with them." Peter didn't even prey,*

he touched the man and healed him because the man had faith and Peter had faith that he can heal because he has spent time meditating, and learning the scriptures to have healing power.

Faith only operates by grace, you have the authority over sickness and disease, have faith and use it.

FAITH.

Genesis 15: 6.NLT

"And Abraham believed the Lord and the Lord counted him righteous because of his faith." Now, I wanted to go back into the beginning up in Genesis. Abraham was an old man and he had no children. He was out of the child bearing age at the time that God promised him that he would have many nations under him, which is family, basically.

Abraham believed the Lord, that is he affirmed that God is dependable. God credited to him as righteous. That is he just or accounted that Abraham measured up to the standard, conformed to the norm. Abraham and God's gracious response to it served as a paradigm of Christian experience in three different new living translations books, Romans, Galatians, and James.

So when you are praying for faith, you're asking God for faith, pray that you believed as Abraham believed. That God give you the faith that Abraham had, to believe the things that you can't see.

Luke 17:6 NLT

> *"He answered, 'If you have faith, even as small as a mustard seed, you could say to this mulberry tree, 'May you be uprooted and thrown into the sea," and it will obey you.'" When you have faith and you believe, you can do anything that you believe in according to God's will.*

Genuine faith is powerful, even in a small quantity. The mustard seed was thought by farmers in the Palestine's to be the smallest of seeds. A mulberry tree has such an extensive and deep root system that it might live for several hundred years. It took a very powerful force to uproot it.

All you have to have faith is as small as a seed to move mountains. That's powerful. So when you're praying, pray this scripture. "Father God, I have the faith of a mustard seed." And believed the things that you are praying for and it shall come to pass according to God's will.

Five and one. "Therefore, we have been made right in God's sight by faith. We have peace with God because of what Jesus Christ, our Lord has done for us." God made us right with him by believing in him and having faith. So if anytime you lack faith, just pray and know that God has made you right. You are right with God through faith.

As long as you believe in God and his principles, you can have whatever it is that you're praying for. And if you lack faith, just remind yourself that Jesus died so that I can have the things that I needed. I shall not lack. I shall not want according to God's will for my life.

Matthew 10:17 NLT

"So faith comes from hearing. That is hearing the good news about Christ." So you must hear God's news, studying, reading, listening to books, listening to tapes. Hear the good news of God to build your faith. Put God's word inside your heart, meditate on it to build faith on God's word and God's promises. So when things come up, you will be ready. You will be built. You will be prepared for whatever obstacles you may face dealing with your faith and challenges in life.

Hebrews 11:1 NLT

"Faith is the confidence that what we hope will actually happen. It gives us assurance about things we cannot see." Faith comes by

the things that we cannot see and we believe that they are here because God gave us these promises that his word is true and faithful. So in order to have faith, you have to believe the things that you cannot see as if they already be.

Hebrews 11: 7-12.NLT

"It is by faith that Noah built a large boat to save his family from the flood. He obeyed God who warned him about the things that had never been before. By his faith, Noah commanded the rest of the world, and he received his righteousness that comes by faith.

It is by faith that Abraham obeyed when God called him to leave home and go to another land that God gave him as his inheritance. He went out knowing where he was going. And even when he reached the land God promised him, he lived there by faith. For he was like a foreigner living in tents. So did Isaac and Jacob and inherited the same promise. Abraham was confidently looking forward to a city with external foundations. A city designed and built by God.

It was by faith that even Sarah was able to have a child. Though she was barren and too old, she believed that God would keep his promise. And so a whole nation came from this one man who was as good as dead. A nation with so many people that like the stars in the sky and the sand on the seashore. There was no way to count them."

When you have faith, God can give you things that you can't even imagine. Abraham and Sarah have faith that God would give them nations of inheritance, of family. From being old and not having any kids at the time, out of age of being able to have kids. But because they have faith, whatever you're going through or whatever you're dealing with, if you have faith, God can move mountains. All it takes is a little bit of faith.

Psalms 25:4 NLT

> *through seven. "Show me the right path, oh God. Point out the road for me to follow. Lead me by your truth and teach me for you are the God who saved me. All day long I put my hope in you. Remember, oh God, your compassion and unfailing love, which you have shown from long ages past. Do not remember the rebellious sins of my youth. Remember me in the light of your unfailing love for you are merciful."*

God is telling us to trust him, to have faith that he will guide us into the right path. Just have faith and trust God. No matter what the situation may be. Have faith and trust God according to his will. He will lead you with knowledge and compassion for you. He loves you. His love never fails. Continue to trust God as you build faith and pray for the things that you are looking for.

FINANCES

Matthew 6: 33 NLT

"Seek the kingdom of God above all else and live righteously and he will give you everything you need. When you put God first in your life, you know that God wants you to be successful. He doesn't want you to hurt or sick but you must trust in him and trust in his will for your life. No matter what the circumstances look like. Learn to trust in God and he will provide everything that you need according to his will, his riches and his glory."

Proverbs 10: 22.NLT

"The blessing of the law makes a person rich and he adds no sorrow. If wealth is gained apart from acknowledgement of God's blessing, often all kinds of struggle accompany. Greedy friends, legal troubles,

fear of loss, and the temptation of pride. God wants you rich, but he also wants you to pray according to his will and God's riches come with no sorrow. You won't have to worry, you won't have to fret. God gives you peace so that you will know that it was a blessing from the law."

2 Corinthians 9:8 NLT

"And God will generously provide all you need. Then you will always have everything you need and plenty left over to share with others. A form of the Greek word for all... A form of the Greek word all is used four times here. Translated every grace, every way, everything you need and every good work. God wants to take care of everything in your life. Trust and have faith."

Deuteronomy 8:18. "Remember the Lord your God, he is the one who gives you power to be successful in order to fulfill the covenant he confirmed to your answers just with an oath. No matter how clever, intelligent, or hardworking that person might be, success flows only from the gracious hand of the Lord. Israel's prosperity must be interpreted as the fulfillment of the ancient promise made to the partial ancestors as part of the covenant blessing. The Lord would lavish upon them. By blessing them in this manner, the Lord will confirm his covenant to Israel. God is confirming his covenant to you that he wants you blessed and he wants you prosperous. Pray, believe and receive."

Philippians 4:19 NLT

"And this same guy who takes care of me will supply all your needs from his glorious riches, which have been given to us in Christ Jesus. God, bountifully blesses those who gives with glorious provision in according to his glory and his purpose. Paul's doxology is based on the ultimate purpose of life to bring glory to God now and forever."

1 Chronicles 29:10-12 NLT

"Then David praised the Lord in the presence of the whole assembly. Oh Lord, the God of our ancestors, Israel. May I be praised forever and ever? Yes. Oh Lord is the greatness, the power of the glory and the victory and the majesty. Everything in heaven and on earth is yours. Oh Lord, this is your kingdom. We adore you as one who is over all things. Wealth and honor come from you alone. For you rule everything power and might are in your hand and at your discretion people are made great and given strength. David's lengthy prayer

began by focusing on God. He did not minimize the gifts of the people, but he knew that their generosity was a product of God's mercy. God wants to be merciful to you and bless you with all kinds of gifts and fruits of the spirit."

Genesis 12:3, NLT

"I will bless those who bless you and curse those who treat you with contempt. All the families on earth will be blessed through you. The Lord spoke to Abraham while he was still in Mesopotamia. God gave Abraham a one verb command with four aspects to it. Abraham was to go out from one, his land, two his relatives and three his father's house, four to the land chosen by God. Obedience to God often means leaving one thing in order to receive something else even better from the Lord."

Luke 16,10-13 NLT

"If you are faithful in the little things, you will be faithful in the large ones, but if you are dishonest in little things, you won't be honest with greater responsibilities. And if you are unworthy about worldly wealth, who trust you with the true riches of heaven? And if you are not faithful with other people's things, why should you be

trusted with things of your own? No one can serve two masters for you will hate one and love the other. You will be devoted to one and despise the other. You cannot serve God and be enslaved to money."

A second lesson that this story teaches is the need to be faithful before the Lord. Spiritually, every believer is a steward of the gifts of God has given. If you are faithful with small amounts of money, the Lord may trust you with much more including things of priceless eternal value. If you can't be trusted with only a little, you would also be a poor steward if more were entrusted to you. Give and you will receive. Your gift will return to you in full. Press down, shaken together to make room for more. Running over and poured into your lap. The amount you give will determine the amount you get back. Measure involves weighing and judging. Be fair to others because the measure you use will return to you. If you are generous, generosity will be returned to you in full measure. If you are stingy and uncharitable such will be the statements, the standards by which you are judged."

Mark 10: 29-30.NLT

"Yes, Jesus replied and I assure that everyone who has given up a house, a brother, a sister, a mother, a father, or

children, or property for my sake and for the good news will receive now in return a hundred times as many houses, brothers, sisters, mothers, children and property along with persecution. And in the world to come, that person will have eternal life. I assure you was Jesus solemn oath formula. He placed equal importance on himself and the gospel. The promise compensation a hundred times more covered this time and the age to come. Following, Jesus provides no protection against suffering, but the reward includes eternal life. The rich ruler sought this but they weren't away from it."

Matthew 6: 19-25.NLT

"Don't store up treasures here on earth where moths eat them and rust destroys them. And where thieves break in and steal. Store Your treasures in heaven where moths and rust cannot destroy and thieves cannot break in and steal. Wherever your treasure is, the desires of your heart will be. Your eye is like a lamp that provides light for your body. When your eye is healthy, your body is filled with light, but when your eye is unhealthy, your body is filled with darkness. And if the light you think you have is actually darkness, how deep that darkness is. No one can serve two masters for you will

hate one and love the other. You will be devoted to one and despise the other. You cannot serve God and his slave to money. This is why I tell you not to worry about everyday life. Whether you have enough food and drink or enough clothes to wear. Life isn't more than food and your body is more than clothing."

Here Jesus emphasizes the fleeting value of worldly wealth. The law of the moth could quickly destroy valuable fabrics that were treasured by ancients. The word rest is literally eating. It can refer to the pitting of metal coins or the vermin of the ruined valuable food stores. Jesus taught that a person's heart truly belongs to what it most treasures. Since a disciple is to love God with all his heart for material possessions and riches is a subtitle form of a dollar tree. In Jewish writing, a good eye represents a generous attitude and a bad eye is stingy, miserably attitude. The bad eye and improper perspective on wealth results in a deep internal darkness. A moral blind is that diminishes the ability to see and pursue what is good.

People have a sinful tendency to make an idol of money which then competes with God for their alliance. Life is more than food, is the rabbinic style argument. It reasons that if God does a greater thing for us, he will also do lesser things. Specifically, if God created you, the greater accomplishment, he is certainly capable of feeding you a lesser accomplishment."

Matthew 13: 23.NLT

"The seed that fell on good soil represents those who truly hear and understand God's word and produce a harvest of 30, 60 or even a hundred times as much as they planted. This parable is frequently interpreted as if the wheat represents true disciples and the weeds represent false disciples, but Jesus interpretation shows that the subject is not the mixture of true or false disciples in the church, but rather the presence of both good and evil in the broader world. Many Jews expected the Messiah to immediately destroyed evil doers and vindict the righteous. Thus they were puzzled so as why Jesus didn't do this if he were truly the son of man.

This parable, Jesus demonstrated that he is not the source of evil. The entire world belongs to the son of man. The devil had no right to do evil intuit. The son of man who has served his kingship over the world by punishing the wicked and blessing the righteous at an appropriate time."

Joshua one and eight. "Study this book of instruction, continuously. Meditate on it day and night, so you will be sure to obey everything written in it. Only then will you prosper and succeed in all you do. More references to the instruction affirm the key importance of God's revelation. Study and learning of it are the form so much a part of one's life. That the words are fully obeyed as in Deuteronomy six, six through nine."

"The frame of God's promise presents in Joshua 1:8 and that indicates that Joshua's success will come because God is with him and they believe him to read and observe God's word."

DISAPPOINTMENT.

1 Peter 5:10-11 NLT

> *"In his kindness, God called you to share in His eternal glory by means of Christ Jesus. So after you suffered a little while, he will restore, support and strengthen you and He will place you on a firm foundation, all power to Him forever. Amen."*

God will strengthen and honor in heaven those who endure suffering for their faith while on earth. No matter what you're going through, just endure because God is your source and He is here to strengthen you and to lift you up through whatever time and disappointment that you may face.

Titus 2:13-14 NLT

> *"While we look forward with hope to that wonderful day when the glory of our great God and savior Jesus Christ will be*

revealed. He gave His life to free us from every kind of sin, to cleanse us and to make us His very own people, totally committed to doing good deeds."

The verb used here for weight often carries a connotation of eagerness. The eager expectation of the return of Christ mentioned here is not to the time of instruction of grace while we wait, it's also the way grace teaches us to renounce sin and live a godly way. Setting our minds on the truth of Christ's return implies us to holiness, the blessing is the appearing of Christ, the reference to Jesus as God and Savior is a strong affirmation of His deity. The phrase, "People for his own possession." translate an unusual phrase with intentional echoes from the Old Testament, Exodus and Malachi. The phrase expresses the sense of prize, treasure, possession. God treasures you and he prizes himself in you.

1 Peter 5:6-7 NLT

"So, humble yourselves under the mighty power of God and at the right time He will lift you up in honor. Give all your worries and cares to God for He cares for you."

Peter encouraged all believers to practice humility and trust God with their cares. Humility commends us to God and fellow humans, which is the opposite effect of arrogance and conceit.

Psalms 34: 17-18.NLT

"The Lord hears His people when they call to Him for help. He rescues them from all their troubles. The Lord is close to the brokenhearted. He rescues those who spirits are crushed."

Broken hearted, and crushed in spirit further develop the image of oppression. Although the emphasis in these terms is on eternal suffering, Yahweh is near those who were broken and humble as opposed to those who have hearts of stone.

Jeremiah 29:11-14 NLT

"'For I know the plans I have for you.', says the Lord. 'They are plans for good, not for despair, to give you a future and a hope. In those days when you pray, I listen. If you look for me wholeheartedly, you will find me. I will be found by you.' says the Lord. 'I will end your capacity and restore your fortunes. I will gather you out of the nations where I sent you and I will bring you home again to your own land.'"

These words are filled with so much faith that no matter what you may be going through, pray and believe, ask God for the strength not to be discouraged, to know that His will will be done and it will be great and marvelous in your life according to his will.

Psalms 30:5 NLT

"For His anger lasts only a moment, but His favor lasts a lifetime. Weeping may last through the night, but joy comes with the morning."

Yes, we may go through trials and difficult times in our life, but God is here to bring us through, to strengthen us, to give us the things that he desires for us. So He allows us to grow through these tough times. So take heed, don't get discouraged. Keep the faith, continue to pray and believe.

DECISIONS

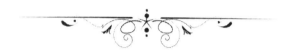

James 1:5 NLT

"If you need wisdom, ask your generous God and he will give it to you. He will not rebuke you for asking."

The world's harsh treatment tempts us to withdraw and refuse to expose our lack of wisdom, for fear of being shamed by our peers. But God gives to all of us generously without criticizing. Thus, he who likes wisdom should ask God freely.

Jeremiah 33:3 NLT

"Ask and I will tell you remarkable secrets you don't know about the things to come."

The things that God will reveal are incomprehensible or inaccessible. That's how great the things are that God will reveal to you when you begin to pray and ask him for his wisdom.

Proverbs 2:6, NLT

"For the Lord grants wisdom. From his mouth comes knowledge and understanding."

Wisdom is not something that a man takes, but that God gives through his Word, which in this case Solomon is inspired to speak.

Proverbs 19:2 NLT

"Enthusiasm without knowledge is no good. Haste makes mistakes."

Take your time and pray and meditate on God's Word and listen. When you pray, you must listen, so God can reveal things to you. Sometimes we begin to rush and we make bad mistakes because it wasn't what God wanted us to do. Slow down, pray and listen.

Proverbs 21:5 NLT

"Good planning and hard work lead to prosperity, but hasty shortcuts lead to poverty."

The reckless person is literally hasty or in a hurry. He likes forethought and diligence.

Proverbs 16:2 NLT

"People may be pure in their own eyes, but the Lord examines their motives."

To evaluate something is to compare it with a standard. If a man's ways are not compared to God's standard, they will seem right or pure, but the Lord evaluates the inner motives, the spirit of men heart and action.

Proverbs 119:105, NLT

> *"Your word is a lamp to guide my feet and a light for my path."*

The lighted path is not whatever we want it to be, but righteous judgments and guides precepts. On such a path, there is no danger or a trap, but a heritage and joy. That's the guidance of the Lord instructions enables the Psalmist to negotiate right and wrong.

Proverbs 18:15 NLT

> *"Intelligent people are always ready to learn. Their ears are open for knowledge."*

Unlike the fool who hates knowledge, refuses to listen and does not intend to by wisdom. The wise seek to hear knowledge and the discerning mind acquires knowledge.

James 1:2-8, NLT

> *"Dear brothers and sisters, when trouble of any kind comes your way, consider it an opportunity of great joy. For now that when your faith is tested, your endurance has a chance to grow, so let it grow. So when your endurance is fully developed, you will be perfect and complete, needing nothing. If*

you need wisdom, ask your generous God and he will give it to you; he will not rebuke you for asking. But when you ask him, be sure that your faith is in God alone. Do not waiver. For a person with divided loyalty is as unsettled as a wave of the sea that is blown and tossed by the wind. Such people should not expect to receive anything from the Lord. Their loyalty is divided between God and the world, and they are unstable in everything that they do. "

The phrase whatever you experience various trials assume that trials are a known part of Christian life. In fact, trials are given for a faithful disciple. The Jewish wisdom tradition held that the experience of trial was proof of a person's faithfulness, joy, suggest and astrological end times hope of deliverance from trials. The joy which a believer endures trials in the present, is a sign of their hope for future relief. Knowing or because you know models, consider in verse two, knowledge that testing of faith produces endurance is the basis for joy. Endurance is the ability to preserve throughout increasing levels of testing [inaudible 00:05:50]. Endurance indicates that further work must be done for the purpose of making the believers mature and complete, lacking nothing.

Immaturity and incompletion are not acceptable longterm states of Christian disciples. The world's harsh treatment tempts us to withdraw and refuse to expose a lack of wisdom for fear of being shamed by our peers. But God gives to all generously and without criticizing. Lest, he who lacks wisdom should ask God freely. A person should ask for wisdom in faith without doubt. The basis for confidence here is not just the fact that we exercise faith, but the person whom we place our faith in, God.

DEPRESSION

2 Samuel 22:29-31 NLT

> *"Oh Lord, you are my lamp. The Lord lights up my darkness. In your strength, I can crush any army. With my God I can scale any wall. God, your way is perfect. All the Lord's promises prove true. He is a shield for all who look to him for protection."*

Both the Lord and his word function as a lamp for his people. David was quick to credit the Lord as the source of his power. God's way, his word, his protection is perfect. David answered his two rhetorical questions quickly. Yahweh was God. The Lord is your rock.

Psalms 34:18 NLT

> *"The Lord is close to the brokenhearted. He rescues those whose spirits are crushed."*

"Brokenhearted" and "crushed in spirit" further develop the image of oppression. Although the emphasis is the term is on eternal suffering, God is near those who are broken and humble as opposed to those who have hearts of stone.

Romans 4:18-22,NLT

"Even when there's no reason for hope, Abraham kept hoping, believing that he would become the father of many nations. For God has sent him. That's how many descendants you will have. And Abraham's faith did not weaken even though at about 100 years of age, he figured his body was as good as dead and so was Sarah's womb Abraham never wavered in believing God's promise. In fact, his faith grew stronger and it has brought glory to God. He was fully convinced that God is able to do whatever he promises, and because of Abraham's faith, God counted him as righteous."

It seemed humanly impossible for Abraham to become a father of many nations when he was old, but he placed his hope in God's promise. Abraham had a realistic evaluation of his prospects for fatherhood. He was about 100 years old and Sarah was childless and long past childbearing years. Yet Abraham did not doubt God's promise and God strengthened his faith. It is Abraham's conviction that God is fully able to do whatever he promised that enabled his faith to overcome the obstacle of the tangible and the visible facts. And this is the kind of faith that receives righteousness.

Revelations 21:4, NLT

> *"He will wipe away tears from their eyes and there will be no more death or sorrow or crying or pain. All these things are gone forever."*

God's presence dwelling with humanity will do away without all death, grief, crying, and pain.

Psalms 40:1-3, NLT

> *"I waited patiently for the Lord to help me and he turned to me and heard my cry. He lifted me out of the pit of despair, out of the mud and out of the mire. He set my feet on solid gold and steadied me as I walked along. He has given me a new song to sing, a hymn of praise to our God. Many will see what he has done and be amazed. They will put their trust in the Lord."*

"Waited patiently" shows faithfulness to God and refrain from taking things into one's own hands or going to another source for help. God is the only source of help for those who trust in him. "Pit" can refer to a deep well. Someone trapped anywhere would probably sink down into the muddy clay and die if someone doesn't pull them out. Figuratively the term is related to [foreign language 00:04:14], representing death. To be brought up needs to be rescued from death. The new song likely refers to the newness of life after being delivered from death.

"But you, oh Lord, are a shield around me. You are my glory. The one who holds my head high."

The image of God as a shield is common, especially in the Psalms. It represents protection during the time of attack. A more unusual deception in identifying God is one of Hebrews words, [foreign language 00:04:52], literally "heavy." It is often used as a person's reputation at significant times being translated as "honor." Its use here seems to indicate that Solomon has found his own significance in honor linked to his relationship with God rather than his own strength.

"Many songs come to the wicked, but unfailing love surround those who trust the Lord." Psalms 32, 19.

The primary reason that although the one who trusts the Lord may find troubles, the Lord's faithful love will always be there.

Romans 8:38-39, NLT

> *"And I am convinced that nothing can ever separate us from God's love. Neither death*

nor life, neither angels nor demons, neither our fears for today nor our worries about tomorrow. Not even the power of the hell can separate us from God's love. No power in the sky above or in the Earth below, indeed nothing in all creation were able to separate us from God's love that is revealed in Christ Jesus, our Lord."

Paul's grand persuasion in this perfect tense, which indicates a past action that has ongoing impact. Having been persuaded by God he stood firm in the belief that nothing could separate him from the love of God. Jesus conquered death and Satan on the cross ensuring that nothing can change God's love or purpose for us. We are protected by God's power through faith, for salvation that is ready to be revealed in the last time.

DOUBT

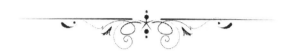

Psalm 77:11-15 NLT: But then I recall all you have done, Oh God, I remember your wonderful deeds of long ago. They are constantly in my thoughts. I cannot stop thinking about your mighty works. Oh God, your ways are Holy. Is there any God as mighty as you? You are the God of great wonders. You demonstrate your awesome power among nations. By your strong arm, you redeem your people, the descendants of Jacob and Joseph. When you are beginning to doubt, remember how mighty God is in your prayers. God is here, and God will create wonders in your life that you cannot begin to imagine long as you trust him. Speak to those mountains and remind them that your God is mighty, and trust him. Don't let doubts overcome your faith.

Isaiah 40:27-28: Oh God, how can you say the Lord does not see your troubles? Oh, Israel, how can you say God ignores your right? Have you ever heard?

Have you ever understood the Lord is everlasting God, the creator of all earth. He never grows weak or weary. No one can measure the depth of his understanding. When Judah experienced God's punishment, Isaiah anticipated that the people would ask why God had abandoned them. The following verses summarize the answers given in part of the chapter. God wanted to deliver his people, and he was fully able to do so. God had the power and wisdom to bring about Judea's deliverance.

James 1:5-7 NLT: if you need wisdom, ask our generous God and he will give it to you. He will not rebuke you for asking. But when you ask him, be sure that your faith is in God alone. Do not waiver, for a person with divided loyalties is as unsettled as a wave of the sea that is blown and tossed by the wind. Such people should not expect to receive anything from God.

The world's harsh treatment temps us to withdraw and refuse to explore our lack of wisdom for fear of being shamed by peers, but God gives us all generously without criticizing. Thus who he lacks wisdom should ask God freely. A person should ask for wisdom and faith without doubting. The basis of confidence here is not just the that we exercise faith, but the person in whom to place our faith.

Psalm 42:11 NLT: Why am I discouraged? Why is my heart so sad? I will put my hope in God. I will praise him again, my Savior and my God.

The Psalmist was speaking of himself. My soul, an attempt to bring comfort and security. In answering the question focusing on depression, he literally commands himself to hope in God. This means waiting on God during the time of crisis, trusting that he will answer your prayers. The point the Psalmist seems to be making is that there is no reason for his depression if God is his savior. In fact, that he repeated this several times there shows the difficulty of initializing the truth.

Genesis 28:15 NLT What's more, I am with you and I will protect you wherever you go. One day I will bring you back to this land. I will not leave you until I have finished giving you everything I have promised.

God is with you and God will honor and praise you no matter what. Don't worry. Don't doubt. God will never leave your side.

Matthew 14:31-33 NLT: Jesus immediately reached out and grabbed him. "You have so little faith," Jesus said. "Why did you doubt me?" When they climbed back in the boat, the wind stopped. Then the disciples worshiped him. "You really are the son of God!" They exclaimed.

You have nothing to worry about. God is with you and God will guide you through everything that you are dealing with. Pray and remember the Scriptures. God will not leave you or forsake you. He is with you to overcome any and everything that you deal with.

John 20:26-29 NLT: Eight days later, the disciples were together again, and this time Thomas was with them. The door was locked, but suddenly as before, Jesus was standing among them. "Peace be with you," he said. Then he said to Thomas, "Put your fingers in here and look at my hands. Put your hands in the wounds in my side. Don't be faithless any longer. Believe." My Lord, my God!" Thomas exclaimed. Then Jesus said to him, "You believe because you have seen. Blessed are those who believe without seeing." Jesus, after eight days refers to the following Sunday. One week after Easter, Jesus condescended to allow Thomas' test of his identity. But when Thomas saw and heard Jesus, no such explanation was necessary. He recognized that in some sense Jesus was God incarnate. The words Lord and God occur together in the Old Testament over 1,000 times. The emperor Domitian also wish to be addressed as our Lord, our God [inaudible 00:06:33]

FORGIVENESS

Psalms 65:3,NLT

"God we are overwhelmed by our sins and you forgive them all."

Anytime that someone has wrong to think about all of the forgiveness that God has given us. I know it may be difficult at times, but think about all the things that we have done and God has forgiven us. Pray God to give us a forgiving heart so that your prayers may be heard. Lord, you are so good. So ready to forgive, so full of unfailing love for all who asks for your help. Pray to the Lord and ask him to forgive you to help you forgive those. He is willing and able to forgive and he is ready.

Psalm 86:5,NLT

"Then I was sprinkled clean water on you and you will be clean. Your filth will be washed away and you will no longer worship idols."

Once the Israelites have arrived in the land, God will sprinkle them with clean water so they will be clean. The figurative language is based on water purification practices. When the priest threw water on persons or objects to cleanse them of purity. Sprinkling them with water or blood symbolizes the cleansing that comes through forgiveness.

Matthew 18:21-35 NLT, parable of the unforgiving debtor.

> *"Then Peter came to ask, Lord, how often should I forgive someone who sins against me? Seven times? No, not even seven. Jesus replied, '77 times.' Therefore, the kingdom of heaven can be compared to the King who decided to bring his accountants up to date, with servants who had borrowed money from him. In the process, one of the debtors brought in who owed millions of dollars, he couldn't pay. So his master ordered that he was sold along with his wife, children and everything that he owned to pay the debt."*

> *"But the man fell down before his master and begged him, 'Please be patient with me and I will pay you.' Then the master was filled with pity for him and he released him and forgave his debt. But when the man left the King, he went to a fellow servant who owed him a few thousands dollars. He*

grabbed him by the throat and demanded instant payment. His fellow servant fell down before him and begged for a little more time. 'Be patient with me and I will pay you.' He pleaded."

"His debtor couldn't wait. He had the man arrested and put in prison until the debt could be paid. When some of the servants saw this, they were very upset. They went to the King and told him everything that had happened. The King called in the man who had forgiven and said, 'You evil servant. I forgave you that tremendous debt because you pleaded with me. Shouldn't you have mercy on your fellow servant just as I had mercy on you?' Then the angry King sent the man to prison to be tortured until he paid his entire debt. That's why my heavenly father will do to you if you refuse to give your brothers and sisters from your heart."

Jesus had promised that the disciples would sit on 12 or ruling over Israel in the Masonic Age. Now, James and John thought, through their mother to gain prominence over their fellows. Along with Peter they were members of Jesus' inner circle because Jesus rebuked Peter they may have inspired a unsprung Peter's position of prominence as well. The cup was a metaphor for suffering. Jesus' question probed the disciples willingness to suffer for him.

Start here. Start here. Although forgiveness, although forgiving someone only seven times seem stingy. This standard was generous considering the fact that rabbis required their students to forgive offenders only three times. Interpreters dispute whether Jesus demanded forgiveness, forgiving one brother 77 times or 490 times, 70 times seven. But Jesus' point was that forgiveness should be unlimited when true repentance is present.

In Jewish parables, the King symbolizes God and settles the account, symbolizing divine judgment. The 10,000 talents was equivalent to a billion in today's dollars. This was more money than was circulating in Palestine. The talent was the largest unit of currency and approximately 6,000 days worth of wages. And 10,000 is the highest single number that can be expressed in Greek, thus we seek that this is the allegory, the sum that represents the sinner's helpless debt to God. Selling the debt towards his family, his positions would hardly began to recoup this debt. Forgiving such a loan is an astonishing act of grace.

100 dinero were equivalent to three months of wages. This was... Point is now revealed. Since, God has shown believers such great mercy by pardoning

their sin they should in return forgive the sins of others of their debt. The word jailers literally means torturers. The debtors torture would continue until the debt was paid in full. Since the debt could not possibly be paid the torture symbolizes eternal punishment.

Colossians 3:13, NLT

> *"Make allowance for each other's faults and forgive anyone who offends you. Remember, the Lord forgave you, so you must forgive others."*

The words accepting and forgiveness express the habitual manner in which believer's exhibit, the stated virtues, both verb, pertinent and interpersonal relationships in the body of Christ. Just as the Lord has forgiven echos Jesus' injunction to forgive because believers are forgiven.

1 John 1:8-9, NLT

> *"If we claim we have no sin we are only fooling ourselves and not living in the truth. But if we confess our sins to him, he is faithful and just to forgive us of our sins and cleanse us of all wickedness."*

In both scripture and church history, people have excused their wrongful deeds by claiming to be right with God. John diagnosed an ancient and recurrent [inaudible 00:07:19] tendency. Confessing our sins does not mean a shallow recruiting of misdeeds. It means owning up to the wrong doing and bringing our lives into line with God's goodness and command. God can forgive and cleanse us of our terrible transgressions.

Ephesians 4:32, NLT

> *"Instead, be kind to others. Tenderhearted, forgiving one another just as God, through Christ has forgiven you." And 37, "Don't judge others and you will not be judged. Don't condemn others or it will all come back against you. Forgive others, and you will be forgiven."*

The problem here are hypocritical judgments, short sighted condemnation, and unforgiving spirit. These warnings do not mean that Jesus followers should not practice careful discernment in judgment.

PATIENCE.

Psalms 75:2 NLT God says,

> *"At the time I have planned, I will bring justice against the wicked."*

Choose a time refers to a set or appointed time, at which, in case God's time for judging. He is orderly in his actions and appointed times for the seasons, the festivals of Israel and final time when we will bring his justice into the world. Be patient. God's timing is always perfect. It might not be when we want it, but God is always right on time.

Proverbs 25: 15.NLT

> *Patience can persuade a prince and a soft speech can break bones.*

A bone is the hardest part of a person. Here it represents the strong resistance of persuasion. Be patient. Whatever you're looking for is coming.

Ecclesiastes 7:8 NLT.

Finishing is better than starting. Patience is better than pride. Be patient and understand that virtue is proved right in the end, and so flee temptations to bribery. Third, abiding anger over current situation in life shows you are a fool.

Ephesians 4:2 NLT.

Always be humble and gentle. Be patient with each other, making allowance for each other's faults because of your love. Humility, gentleness and patience are absolutely an essential if unity is to be maintained.

1 Corinthians 13 4-5 NLT.

Love is patient and kind. Love is not jealous or boastful or proud or rude. It doesn't demand its own way. It is not irritable and it keeps no record of being wrong. Be patient. Love one another.

Proverbs 14: 29.NLT

People with understanding control their anger, a hot temper shows great foolishness. Patience is literally slow to become angry. Outside of Proverbs the phrase is always used of that in the Old Testament. Be slow to anger. Be patient.

Psalms 37:7 NLT.

Be still in the presence of the Lord and wait patiently for him to act. Don't worry about evil people who prosper or fret about their wicked schemes. Be solid is a command similar to being quiet before the Lord. Sometimes it is the result of discipline, but here it means to wait on the Lord instead of acting on one's own.

Psalms 27: 14.NLT

Wait patiently for the Lord. Be brave and courageous. Yes. Wait patiently for the Lord. Waiting for the Lord is an abbreviated way to express waiting for an answer to prayer. Rather than taking matters into your own hands, the people of God should wait patiently for God's response.

GUIDANCE

Psalms 25:4-5, NLT

> *"Show me the right path, O Lord. Point out the road for me to follow. Lead me by your truth and teach me for you are the God who saves me. All day long I put my hope in you."*

God and teach are essentially synonymous in this text. They refer to God's directing those who are faithful to Him. His truth is the guide for our lives. The paths are similar to ways in verse 10 and are connected, not only to God's truth, but to also God's faithfulness in love.

Psalm 32:8 NLT. The Lord says,

> *"I will guide you along the best path for your life. I will advise you and watch over you."*

This is a wisdom section in the Psalms as evidence by the term instruct and counsel. This might be related to designated and [inaudible 00:01:06]. A horse and a mule need to be controlled in order to be useful to people. Otherwise, they are too outstanding, will not obey the master. In the human world, they are the best compared to fools.

Proverbs 3:5-6.NLT

> *"I lay down and slept, yet I woke up in safety for the Lord was watching over me. I am not afraid of 10,000 enemies who surround me on every side."*

To lie down and to sleep are poetic and tangible ways to describe a state of security. Only a person who feels secure will be able to sleep, undisturbed by troubling thoughts. Psalm 4:8 uses the same combination of verbs, added in the phrase, the Psalmist was confident that he would wake again because it is God himself who sustained him. The Psalm's security was unrelated to the circumstances even though he was surrounded by enemies. Confidence in God's protection does not depend on one enemies circumstances.

Isaiah 30:21,

> *"Your own ears will hear him. Right behind a voice will say, this is the way you should go, whether to the right or to the left."*

Walking in the way in resent, reminiscent of the language of the Psalms 1, and Proverbs. There are two ways, a crooked path that represents an evil life heading towards death and straight to the path of godliness that leads to life.

Isaiah 58:11,NLT "

> *The Lord will guide you continually, giving you water when you are dry and restoring your strength. You will be like a well-watered garden, like an even flowing spring.* "

The onlooker looks forward to the restoration when God's people will leave their captivity and return for the land, but the land and the cities, especially Jerusalem will be in ruins. Obedience will lead to prosperity and fertility. The parsed land will turn into a watered garden. Obedience and true pity will also lead to the strength needed to rebuild the city in Jerusalem and its defenses.

John 14:26, NLT

> *"But when the father sends the advocate as my representative, that's it. The Holy spirit, he will teach you everything and he will remind you of everything I have told you."*

John 16:3 NLT

"When the Spirit of truth comes, he will guide you into our truth. He will not speak on his own but he will tell you what he has heard. He will tell you about the future."

The Spirit's ministry of guiding Jesus followers in all the truth will fulfill the souls longing for divine guidance. Isaiah recounted how God led his people into the wilderness by the Holy spirit and predicted guides with new guidance in the future. The word declare occurs more than 40 times in the book of Isaiah where declaring things to come is said to be the exclusive domain of God and what God challenges pretend is to declare the thing to come.

STRESS.

Luke 12:25 through 26 NLT.

"Can all your worries add a single moment to your life?

And if worry can't accomplish a little thing like that, what's the use of worrying over bigger things?"

Jesus' advice his disciples was not to be overcome with anxiety over the basic needs of life. Worry can't change even the little things, since God feeds the ravens who has no storeroom, he will not care for humans his most valuable, beloved creatures?

Psalm 62:1-8 NLT.

"I wait quietly before God, for my victory comes from him.

He alone is my rock and my salvation, my fortress where I will never be shaken.

So many enemies against one man - All of them trying to kill me. To them, I'm just a broken-down wall or a tottering fence.

They plan to topple me from my high position. they delight in telling lies about me. They praise me to my face but curse me in their hearts.

Let all that I am wait quietly before God, for my hope is in him.

He alone is my rock and my salvation, my fortress where I am not shaken.

My victory and honor come from God alone. He is my refuge, a rock where no enemy can reach me.

O my people, trust in him at all times. Pour out your heart to him, for God is our refuge."

Psalm 69:1-36 NLT.

"Save me, O God, for the floodwaters are up to my neck.

Deeper and deeper I sink into the mire; I can't find a foothold. I am in deep water, and the floods overwhelm me.

I am exhausted from crying for help; my throat is parched. My eyes are swollen with weeping, waiting for my God to help me.

Those who hate me without cause outnumber the hairs on my head. My enemies try to destroy me with lies, demanding that I give back what I didn't steal.

O God, you know how foolish I am; my sins cannot be hidden.

Don't let those who trust in you be ashamed because of me, O sovereign Lord of Heaven's Armies. Don't let me cause them to be humiliated, O God of Israel.

For I endure insults for your sake, humiliation is written all over your face.

Even my own brothers pretend they don't know me; they treat me like a stranger.

Passion for your house has consumed me, and the insults of those who insult you have fallen on me.

When I weep and fast, they scoff at me.

When I dress in burlap to show sorrow, they make fun of me.

I am the favorite topic of town gossip, and all drunks sing about me.

But I keep praying to you, Lord, hoping this time you will show me favor. In your unfailing love, O God, answer my prayer with your sure salvation.

Rescue me from the mud; don't let me sink any deeper! Save me from those who hate me, and pull me from these deep waters.

Don't let the floods overwhelm me, or the deep water swallow me, or the pit of death devour me.

Answer me, O God, for your unfailing love is wonderful. Take care of me, for your mercy is plentiful.

Don't hide from your servant; answer me quickly, for I am deep in trouble!

Come and redeem me; free me from my enemies.

You know my shame, scorn and disgrace. You see all my enemies are doing.

Their insults have broken my heart, and I am in despair. If only one person would show pity; if only one would turn and comfort me.

But instead, they give me poison for food; they offer me sour wine for my thirst.

Let the bountiful table set before them become a snare and their prosperity become a trap.

Let their eyes go blind so they can't see, and make their bodies shake continually.

Pour out your fury on them; consume them with your burning anger.

Let their homes become desolate and there tents be deserted.

To the one you have punished, they add insult to injury; they add to the pain of those you have hurt.

Pile their sins up, and don't let them go free.

Erase their names from the Book of Life; don't let them be counted among the righteous.

I am suffering and in pain. Rescue me, O God, by your saving power.

Then I will praise God's name by singing, and I will honor him with Thanksgiving.

For this will praise the Lord more than sacrificing cattle, more than presenting a bull with horns or hooves.

The humble will see their God at work and be glad. Let all who seek God's help be encouraged.

For the Lord hears the cries of the needy; he does not despise his imprisoned people.

Praise him, O heavens and earth, the seas and all in them.

For God will save Jerusalem and rebuild the towns of Judah. His people will live there and settle in their land.

The descendants of those who obey him will inherit the land, and those who love him will live there safely."

Isaiah 40:30 through 31 NLT.

"Even youths will become weak and tired, and young men will fall in exhaustion.

But those who trust in the Lord will find new strength. They soar high on wings like eagles. They will run and not grow weary. They will walk and not faint."

God not only has strength, but he distributed the strength to his people. The criteria for receiving God's strength was not youth, but trust. Those who trusted God would have unlimited source of strength."

2 Corinthians 4:8-12.NLT

"We are pressed on every side by troubles, but we are not crushed. We are perplexed, but not driven to despair.

We are hunted down, but never abandoned by God. We get knocked down, but we are not destroyed.

Through suffering, our bodies continue to share in the death of Jesus so that the life of Jesus may also be seen in our bodies.

Yes, we live under constant danger of death because we serve Jesus, so that the life of Jesus will be evident in our dying bodies.

So, we live in the face of death, but this has resulted in eternal life."

Philippians 4:4 through nine.NLT

"Always be joyful in the Lord. I say it again-rejoice!

Let everyone see that you are considerate in all you do. Remember, the Lord is coming.

Don't worry about anything; instead, pray about everything. Tell God what you need and thank him for all he has done.

Then you will receive God's peace, which exceeds anything we can understand. His peace will guard your hearts and minds as you live in Christ.

And now, dear brothers and sisters, one final thing. Fix your thoughts on what is true, and honorable, and right, and pure, and lovely, and admirable. Think about things that are excellent and worthy of praise.

Keep putting into practice all you learned and received from me-everything you heard from me and saw me doing. Then the God of peace will be with you."

WISDOM.

Proverbs 1-7.NLT

Fear of the Lord is the foundation of true knowledge but fools despise wisdom and discipline. The fear of the Lord involves all reverence, love and trusting God. It accomplishes knowledge, humility, obedience and blessing. The beginning is what we must come first. The prerequisite. It is also the chief response to supreme principle. All three kind of fool or outstandingly immoral. The fool, the word steady is self-sufficient and he tests the wisdom of any advice or corrections.

Proverbs 2: 6-12.NLT

For The Lord grants wisdom. From his mouth come knowledge and understanding. He grants a treasure of common sense to the honest, he's the shield to those who walk in integrity. He guards the path of the just and protects those who are faithful to him. Then you will understand what is right, just and fair and he will find the right way to go. For wisdom will enter your heart and knowledge will fill you with joy. Wise choices will watch over you. Understand you will, understanding will keep you safe. Wisdom will save you from evil people from those who words are twisted. Wisdom is not something a man takes, but that God gives through his word, which in this case Solomon inspired to speak. As we store up God's commandments, he stores of success is our reward. Success is competence. Our sound judgment upright means corresponding to God's economic ethical instruction. The Hebrew word for integrity implies genuineness and reliability. It also is translated honorable and honest.

Proverbs 13-10.NLT

> *Pride leads to conflict. Those who take advice are wise. Arrogance here contracts with those who take advice. So an arrogant person is viewed as a know it all.*

Matthew 7:24 through 27.NLT

> *Anyone who listens to my teachers and follows it is wise like a person who builds a house on solid rock. Though the rain comes in torrents and the flood waters rise and the winds beat against the house. It won't*

collapse because it is built on bare rock. But anyone who hears my teaching and does not obey it is foolish. Like a person who builds a house on sand. When the rain and floods come and the winds beat against the house, it will collapse. Collapse with a mighty crash. The adjectives sensible and foolish describe a person's spiritual and moral state, not his intellect, whether one is considered sensible or foolish is determined by his response to Jesus' teaching. Since old Testament writers describe God's wrath using the image of a great storm, the storm that destroys the house on the sand is a picture of a divine judgment. Hence the person who hears an X on Jesus' teaching is prepared for judgment. The one who hears but doesn't act on Jesus' word will be destroyed in the storm of judgment.

1 Corinthians 2:1-16 NLT

When I first came to you, dear brothers and sisters, I didn't use lofty words and impressive wisdom to tell you God's secret plan. For I decided that I will, that while I was with you, I would forget everything except Jesus Christ, the one who was crucified. I came to you when weakness, intimid, and trembling, and my message and my preaching was very plain. Rather than using clever and precise speeches, I relied on the power of the Holy Spirit.

I did this so you would trust in my human wisdom, but not in my human wisdom, but in the power of God. Yet when I was among mature believers, I do speak with words of wisdom, but not the kind of wisdom that belongs to this world or to the rulers of this world who are assumed forgotten. No, the wisdom we speak of is the mystery of God. His plan that was previously hidden, even though he made it for our ultimate glory before the world began, but the rulers of this world have not understood it. If they had, they would not have crucified our glorious Lord. That is what the scriptures mean when they say no eyes had seen, no ears have heard and no mind has imagined what God has prepared for those who love him. But it was to us that God revealed these things by his spirit, for the spirit searches out everything. It shows as God's deepest secret, no one can know a person's thought except the person's own spirit. No one can know God's thought except God's own spirit.

And we received God's spirit, not the world's spirit. So we can know the wonderful things God has freely given us. When we tell you these things, we do not use words that come from human wisdom. Instead we speak words given to us by the spirit, using the spirit's words to explain spiritual truth, but the people aren't spiritual. We can't receive these truths from God's spirit. It all sound foolish to them and they can't understand, for only those who are spiritual can understand the spirit. Mean, what the spirit means. Those who are spiritual can evaluate all things, but they themselves can not be evaluated by others for who can know the laws, thoughts, who knows enough to teach him, but we understand these things for we have the mind of Christ.

Proverbs 4:6-7 NLT.

> *Don't turn your back on wisdom for she will protect you, love her and she will guard you. Getting wisdom is the wisest thing you can do and whatever else you do, develop good judgment.*

There's a great emphasis here that wisdom and understanding of the most important acquisitions literally in all your purchasing, purchase understanding. That is, spend all your assets on understanding. Supreme could also mean the beginning. The first thing to get as with salvation, the cost of godly wisdom is not silver or gold. Whether a person must stop desiring anything else and love, cherish, and embrace only the one thing that is part of what it means to give up one's life for something.

PEACE.

Psalms 34:14, NLT

> *"Turn away from evil and do good search for peace and work to maintain peace."*

Isaiah 53:5, NLT

> *"But he was pierced for our rebellion, crushed for our sins. He was beaten so we could be whole. He was whipped so we could be healed."*

Jesus suffered the ultimate sacrifice so that we can walk in peace and love amongst each other. Have peace the peace that God has given us.

Matthew 5:23-26, NLT

> *"So if you are presenting a sacrifice at the altar in the temple and you suddenly remember that someone has something against you, leave your sacrifice there at the altar. Go and reconcile to that person, then*

come and offer your sacrifice. When you are on your way to court with your adversary settle your differences quickly. Your accuser may hand you over to the judge who will hand you over to an officer, who will be thrown into prison. And if that happens, you surely won't be free again until you have paid every last penny."

Disciples must attempt at their earliest opportunity to reconcile with a brother or a sister who has something against them, even if doing so interrupt the business. Speaking to the context of his day, Jesus said to the disciples, should seek reconciliation even if it meant halting in the middle of offering sacrifices at Jerusalem temple. This interruption was significant since Jesus original audience located away from Jerusalem would have to abandon their gift at the altar, travel four days to reach Galilee and seek reconciliation, then return to Judah to complete the sacrifice. Such is a priority of reconciliation. I personally typically pay a similar penalty for their offenses by seeking an out of court settlement rather than waiting for the issue to be settled in court. This illustrates that reconciliation is urgent because the longer it is postponed, the more severe the consequences.

John 14:27, NLT

"I am leaving you with a gift, peace of mind and heart and the peace I give you is a gift that the world cannot give. So, don't be troubled or afraid."

The expression peace could serve as a reading or announced blessing upon those who enjoy right relationship with God. The Old Testament prophet, a period of peace following Messiah's coming for he is the prince of peace who will proclaim peace to all nations. There will be tiding of peace and salvation and God will establish an everlasting covenant of peace with his people. Jesus, pouring an encouragement for his followers not to be troubled or fear, echos Moses parting counsel.

Philippians 4:4-7,NLT

"I will be full of joy in the Lord, I say it again. Rejoice. Let everyone see that you are considerate in all you do. Remember the Lord is coming. Don't worry about anything. Instead, pray about everything. Tell God what you need and thank him for all he has done. Then you will experience God's peace which exceeds anything we can understand. His peace will guard your heart and mind as you live in Christ Jesus."

Paul approached peace from two perspectives. Peace with troublesome circumstances and constructing an environment of peace. Graciousness implies selflessness and respect for others. Seldom mentioned in Paul's writing. Graciousness is expected of believers and Christian leaders, indicates it is part of a church reputation. The Lord is near reminded the Philippians believers of Christ unseen peace, worry and anxiety, prayer is the antidote for worry. Three words express different aspects of prayer. Prayer is a worship attitude, petition a need and request the specific concern. Thanksgiving shapes prayers with gratitude in response to the peace of God brings power to endure. The peace surpasses knowledge claiming a troubling situation when explanations fail.

Further, peace of God by keeping anxieties from hearts. Choose, it's heart's choices and minds attitudes.

Colossians 3:15, NLT

"And let the peace that comes from Christ rule in your heart. For as members of one body, you are called to live in peace and always be thankful."

The peace brought by Christ should control believers' hearts. Be thankful, harks back.

Hebrews 12:14 NLT

"Work at living in peace with everyone and work at living a Holy life. For those who are not Holy will not see the Lord."

The sovereign grace of the father display in discipline is the source from which Christian find strength to move forward.

Salvation is by grace, but it demands a human response. Loving discipline is evidence of the father's grace and his children, [inaudible 00:06:04] hold on to grace. Christian should move towards peace and holiness and they should warn one another against falling short of God's grace or allowing a root of bitterness to spring up within them. The church does not exist on Mount Sinai with terrifying law that commands and condemns. Rather, the church is moving towards Mount Zion, where it should dwell in the presence of God. Jesus, angels and righteous people who have been perfected by the sprinkled blood of Christ.

1 Peter 5:7, NLT

"Give all your worries and cares God for he cares about you."

Peter and [inaudible 00:06:46] are believers to practice humility and trust God with their cares. Humility can commend us to God and fellow humans, which is the opposite effect of arrogance and conceit.

Made in the USA
Columbia, SC
11 March 2023

13567925R00076